Bags of Life
SOLILOQUIES OF A SOLUS SAG

Copyright © 2018 Charlene Howard

All rights reserved.

ISBN-10: 1720910413

ISBN-13: 978-1720910411

Cover By: Xavier Faust

Dedication

This book is dedicated to anyone who has ever felt broken and alone. To my daughter Nala & my son Nolan, that you learn from my lessons and that you never limit yourself or your thinking. You will live a life full of laughter and love. To all the people especially men that hurt me….. Bless You!

Acknowledgements

Many people have impacted my life to be able to write this book and I thank you. There are some very special people that without you I may have never accomplished this dream. I would like to thank Ms. Cynthia Lamb, You inspired me and gave me the confidence to move forward. I would also like to thank Shayla (Atkins) Baxter, Shayla Burton, Perry Marrow Jr., Renaldo Slaughter and Justin Warren.

Table of Contents

Introduction..8-12

A SOLUS SAG..13

After the storm...14

Beasty Beauty..15

BELIEVE...16

Butterfly..17

Closed Doors...18

Cloudy Heart..19

Cover Girl..20

Cycles...21

Daybreak...22

Diaries of a Broken Sag 23-27

Disillusionment..28

Distorted to Delivered......................................29

Emotion..30

Every Morning...31

Table of Contents (Cont'd)

Finding Home 32

Forever. Never. Ever. 33

Forsaken Shoulder 34

Fractured 35

GOAL Digger 36

Hide away 37

His Heart Speaks 38

Human Perspective 39

Inconsolable 40-42

Inspired Spirit 43

Jaded 44

KNEW ART, NEW HEART 45

Legal Thoughts 46

Love Imposter 47

Lost Soul 48-49

Misguided Judgement 50

Table of Contents (Cont'd)

Neglected Abandonment 51

Obscure Liberation...52

Phoenix..53

Queen Status..54

Real False..55

Rested Peace..56

Sag Tamed..57-58

Served Notice..59-60

Similarly Different...61

Tell...62-63

Thinking Thoughts...64

This, That, It... Deal! 65

Uninhabited 66-68

Unfelt 69

Unspoken Unity 70

Wasted time...71

Zealous Exhalation 72-74

Introduction

Tonight, I am sitting under the covers of my queen-sized bed after a day in the emergency room; despite my constant physical pain, it is only a representation of the depths of the internalization of the pain I am enduring. I am sitting here in the dark as usual. Alone better yet SOLUS!

There are many places that I often drift away to and gather my mental thoughts. I take long drives, long walks to and around the parks or lakes. Sometimes, I lay in the middle of my closet floor, but today, I choose to sit in my bedroom. The bedroom is one of the most intimate places in a person's home, and if you are reading this collection, I am choosing to share some of my most intimate moments.

Today, I am filled with emotions with no one to express them to but me. This internal discussion seems to be my norm. I become angry, I become sad, I become emotional; whatever I become, there is often a thought associated with what I am feeling. Very

Introduction (Cont'd)

much like you, you may have thoughts too. How often do you share your thoughts? Who do you tend to talk to about what is going on in your head? Maybe you talk to a friend or family member. Maybe your pastor or your counselor. If you are like me, self-talk seems to be the continuous talk. Talking to yourself sounds a bit bizarre; however, at times, it could be the very remedy you need.

I accept as true that getting my emotions and my feelings out in an appropriate way is a healthy expression of self-love. Too frequently we go through our daily lives with bottled-up emotions, holding on to negative spirits and mental processes and internal pain. There are even times that we find ourselves in a good mental state with good things to express, yet we have no one to share them with. There are also instances when we do find a person to talk to; they do not seem as happy as we are about the news we have to share. I understand it all.

Introduction (Cont'd)

This book is one of the Bags of Life series entitled Soliloquies of a Solus Sag. I am a Sagittarius, born on December 9, 1982. I am a Sagittarius through and through. I do not wake up every morning and read my horoscope to determine my life doings, but if researched, I would say that I am the description of what a Sagittarius would be.

We are said to be very passionate, expressive individuals. We are in love with freedom and speaking our minds as it comes to us. We have harsh words with good intentions and good hearts, but sometimes, people are not able to handle us and do not understand how we operate or what we need. We are honest, we are loyal, and we care. We are impatient and the petty of the petty. We are very impulsive in nature, and we love to go with the flow. When people make us feel restrained, judged or misunderstood, we will shut down, disappear and become unemotional, yet all the time we are the opposite, well at least I am. I want to reach out. I want to be

Introduction (Cont'd)

around and love and be loved. I want to be understood or at least I used to.

Now, I just want to share with others my feelings, my truth, my soliloquies: the thoughts that I have aloud, the thoughts that I keep to myself. Regardless of whether anyone hears me, regardless of whether anyone understands, I want to share them because I no longer want to just be understood but want others to feel understood and to show others that no matter what they may be going through, someone else may be too, and there are positive ways to release the feelings and emotions that you may feel you cannot say or share with others.

I want you to know that the things that I feel and think are not just for myself but for the healing of others, for others to take the time and think. I want you to reflect on your thoughts maybe think about your loved ones, your friends, even your enemies, and consider, maybe, they have these thoughts as well, or even consider, what thoughts that others might have that keep them in

Introduction (Cont'd)

bondage or fear because of what people might think of them. What might keep them sitting in their room, in the dark? Alone? Let's take this journey and unpack these thoughts as I reveal the soliloquies of a solu sag. My soliloquies.

A SOLUS SAG

I want to
talk to you
actually talk
to you with hopes
you will talk back
but instead of talk back
I get fall back
so I fall back
and let my pen
meet paper
my only true audience
audience of one
where it should have
been two
It should have
been you
but instead
It's paper
It's pen
Finding myself
here by myself
again.

After the storm

I believe that you are sorry.
But I am just afraid.
Afraid to talk to you.
Afraid to make you mad.
Afraid to say the wrong thing the wrong way.

I am so hurt.
Dealing with so much pain.
No one to talk to.
Asking God what did I do?
Believing I deserved the blow.

Now trying to find a way to trust.
Hoping it will never happen again.
Finding a way to find a place of peace.

I would've rather dealt with you cheating on me than this.

Beasty Beauty

Everyone expects
a woman to be loving.
Soft and kind almost
Like rose petals or
Cherry blossoms.

But what happens
When beauty,
Is really the beast?

I have not been
Your typical woman
Of dazzling me with jewelry
And flowers.
Call me cynical but
It's a behavior of a
Fabricated fantasy.

But how did this happen?
When did I
Get this way?

Cause it doesn't seem natural.
It doesn't seem normal.
I've never been normal.

A woman should be the
Object of her loves affection
But sometimes there is a beast
Within every woman
That if not tamed or controlled
Will destroy everything around him.

BELIEVE

Dear Doubt;

Better yourself with each new arisen sun.

Expanding your thinking creates growth.

Love is a medicine for your healing.

Inside you will find your inspiration.

Exhalation is needed to renew your soul.

Victory belongs to the visionary.

Enjoyment of living is key to your success.

Sincerely, BELIEVE!!

Butterfly

I wonder
what a butterfly said
before it had wings?

I wonder
If someone told it
that it would go
Through an identity crisis.

I wonder
If the butterfly
Cared about being
A butterfly at all?

I never knew
I would have wings.
I never knew that I would change.
I did know I would be great one day.

So I tell you.
It's ok to not know.
It's ok to be alone.
For by myself I got my wings.

One day I stopped eating.
And my whole world seem to turn.
It's when it looks most bleak to you,
That you will transform too.

Closed Doors

I saw a door,
It was closed.
I knocked.
It was opened.

It wasn't long,
Before that open door,
Was shut once again.

I saw a door,
It was open.
I walked towards,
It was closed in my face.

It wasn't long,
Before open doors,
Kept closing.

It wasn't long,
Before closed doors,
Stopped opening.

I saw no door.
I saw no way.
I built my own door.
I built my own way.

If one door closes,
Build your own.

Cloudy Heart

As he grows old,

His heart turns cold.

Not any temperature,

but frostbite potential.

And his emotions stay mental,

Lacking the physical.

Blocked by wants and fears,

Blocked by pride and held back tears.

Written on the lines is his heart,

Worn in his eyes are his feelings.

But he just don't know how to cry,

He'd be lying if he said he tried.

These are his confessions,

Just learned a couple lessons,

Now he has lost all his possessions.

Cover Girl

Hey Girl!

Why you have to cover?

Girl?

Your face looks a mess

But no one really sees it.

Because you are covered.

Lipstick of deceit that plagues your mind,

The eyeshadow stroke to cover up the pain,

The foundation of masking hurt.

Yet all that cover, girl

You never realized that everything you held

Was uncovered in your eyes.

You can't cover girl.

Cycles

I'm Tired!
Tired of the same cycle.
Learn me,
Like me,
Love me, well
What feels like love until?
It all crumbles
Down to a
Lie that leaves me.
Leaves me
Alone,
Abandoned,
A broken Heart,
A Restless Spirit.
A Spirit that yearns
To live a life of
Love and Laughter
but love only turns
To bitterness
And hate that makes
My spirit yearn for the
Moment you will leave me.
That the lie
crumbles down
it was never you.
I
Never
Loved me
Liked me
Learned me.
Cycles
I'm Tired of.

Daybreak
Break away from the day.
Take the time to feel the rays,
As the day beaks,
Don't let it
Break your day.
For today
Is another day,
Of Daybreak.

Diaries of a Broken Sag

09.21.2016

Anxiety is my biggest problem.

Carrying everyone is what I do.

But I can't carry myself.

And no one carries me.

I don't like asking for help.

People will use it against you.

Friendly with everyone.

Friends with no one.

Diaries of a Broken Sag (Cont'd)

09-22-2016

Spiraling into an abyss of self-destruction. Wondering when the storms are going to end. When the pain will cease. See I know I haven't been the best, made the best, acted the best nor am I the worst or been the worst. I mean not to stroke my ego but I considered myself a pretty good human being. I try not to hate, I help all I can, sometimes more than I should, but yet there seems to be an everlasting shadow overtaking my life. The on gleam of light is exasperated by darkness. Emotional thunder rolls, while the mental break strikes me down overbearing the entity that is me. Who is me? I just want this everlasting storm to end. My thoughts to stop. The noise to clear. The sounding, pounding of the internal spiraling abyss to self-destruction.

Life Unfulfilled. They say good things happen to good people. Well does that mean I am bad? Because all I've been getting is bad things. Bad things happen to me continuously. One after another. I'm just drowning. I have no umbrella. No energy to leave the storm cause once this storm ends. The next one quickly begins and I'm back can't see beginning from end.

Diaries of a Broken Sag (Cont'd)

09.28.2016

I feel blah. Trying to get out these up and down moments.

*Failure
*Broke
*Lonely
*Sad
*Depressed

Not focused. Nothing gets done.
Emotionally frustrated all the time.

Yet I have to smile to keep from crying.

10.23.2017

I don't feel anyone understands what all I deal with and have to do. My life feels so disconnected and I am overwhelmed. I feel like the mirror shattered and I'm picking up the pieces trying to put them back together but instead of it feeling like it used to be. It feels different and strange. I feel like I am losing my sanity, respect, love. I usually keep my life separate but now it's finding my identity. How they come together or stay apart.

Diaries of a Broken Sag (Cont'd)

11.6.2017

Today
Was a
Very
Bad day.
☹

I'm totally broken on the inside; I
*My mind is gone
*My body hurts

11.12.2017

I'm Scared
But have no one
To talk to.
     I'm Alone

11.23.2017

Worst
Thanksgiving
Ever

Alone, Scared, Can't Sleep, Anxious & Depressed.

11.26.2017

I've been praying. I can't deal with everything.
I'm failing school. I'm broke financially and
I'm emotionally wounded.
I had to make a choice for my sanity

Diaries of a Broken Sag (Cont'd)

12.09.2017

It's my birthday,
The worst birthday.
I have a home going to attend
Beoncka passed away
And I don't understand why.

I am already depressed.
Going won't be best.

It's my birthday
I'm sick
I'm hurt
I'm home
Alone

It's my birthday,
Worst birthday ever.

12.10.2017

This day I will never forget.
This day was unexpected.

Thanks
J&J

01.05.2018

December was a blur.
Went by slow and quick
I have to move on
Mentally, physically & emotionally.

Disillusionment

When I met you I was angry.
My anger turned to fear.

Developing a guarded heart.
Building up my wall of china.

I would give away my all.
I would give away everything.

Whatever I thought could make him happy.
To make him a better man.

Because of this I lost everything.
Everything that I rebuilt was gone again.

Left in a place of disparity and desperation.
A place of disillusionment.

Distorted to Delivered

I thought it was a dream,
But more like distorted reality.
Distracted by your movement.
Delaying me from true destiny.

Chasing after what I thought
Looked like destiny.
Only to stop at the road of
Deception and Deceit.

Distraction was your method.
Deception was your poison.
Destruction was your objective.
Defaming was your goal.

I know it's not a dream.
This may be a distorted reality but
You will no longer distract.
Your deception can't destroy or defame.

Focus is my method.
Forgiveness is my poison.
Future is my objective.
Freedom is my goal.

Emotion

The basis of my emotions
Is the emotion
Of an emotion.
That's like the ocean
Large and endless.

An emotion so deep.
Making me lose sleep.
Was an emotion that creep.
It was almost like it leaped.

Revealed was an emotion
With no awareness of the emotion.
The emotion that leaped.
An emotion that creep.
Constant loss of sleep.
This emotion is too deep.
Too large and endless
Like the ocean.

An emotion.
The emotion.
The basis of my emotion.

Every Morning

Every morning she wakes
She wonders.
When the dream will end
And a nightmare start again.

She longs to hear his voice.
To calm her anxiousness.
The thought of his touch
Easing her pain.

If only she wasn't so broken inside.
If only she could be vulnerable again.
Will she ever be unbroken?
Will she ever open up?

The pain of loving him,
Is her nightmare.
It started when she thought,
The dream would end.
The nightmare starts,
Every morning
She wakes without him.

Every night she dreams.
Every morning it ends.
And the cycle starts
All over again.

Finding Home

Some people say home is not a place, it's a feeling.
They say home is where the heart is.
Others say home is made of hopes and dreams.

I remember Dorothy and her red slippers say
"There's no place like home"

Hearing the voice of Luther Vandross sing
"A house is not a home when there's no on there to
hold you tight"

Home is the place of happiness.
The place where joy is filled and passion ignites your soul.
A place where you are able to let the laughter go.

Home is the place of opportunity.
The place where you are open and true to be you.
A place where you are able to make mistakes and grow.

Home is the place of meditation.
The place where you can reflect and learn self-mediation.
A place where you are able to be self-aware and glow.

Home is the place of empowerment.
The place where you are encouraged and to be refreshed.
A place where you are able to let thoughts flow.

Where you find:
    Happiness
      Opportunity
     Meditation
        Empowerment

You find **HOME.**

Forever. Never. Ever.

It was all a dream, more like mare of dreams.

A nightmare!

Waking intensively from what I thought was
Forever.

It should've been never, they say never say never
But in this case
Never.

The dream that was reality fades away.
The pain remains, the memory engrained.
Awake I see this dream. Sleep walking without sleep.

How can I awaken from this mare of dreams?

This nightmare!

The dream that is in my slumber.
The dream that is in my awakened reality.
That dream that should've been
Never

Thinking this would last
Forever.

But all I want now is to forget. Will I
Ever?

Forsaken Shoulder

I am scared
with no one
to talk to
with no one
to hear me
I am alone.

See people say
call me
talk to me
but when you
have fear
all that is hazed.

Cause
you remember
the last time
you called
the last time
you talked.

Your words
became their
avenue to judge
so you
stop calling
so you
stop talking.

I am scared
with no one
to talk to
with no one
to hear me
I am alone.

Fractured

Just when you
Thought,
you have dealt
with it all.

Sitting, thinking
of all you endured.
Pain and Sadness.
but never fear,
not a fear like this.

It was November Six,
I will never forget.
I ended that day,
Full of regret.

What seem
to be a threat.
Became a
downward spiral
of unforeseen reality.

Mind Forgotten,
      Eyes Teared,
           Mouth Silenced,
                  Hands Shaking,
                        Body Bruised,
                              Soul Broken.

GOAL Digger

She is a goal digger.
Not a gold digger.

Looking for the one
Growing,
Looking for the one
Open,
Not settling for stagnation but
Ability for action.
Looking for the one that
Learned to learn.

She ain't no gold digger.
She's a goal digger.

Hide away

She remembered the days
When she looked in the mirror
And the woman she seen
looking back at her was beautiful
outside but dying on the inside.

Never been abused or
Hurt or talked about
At least that's what
She made herself think.

A pain so deep
Only a savior could see
Hidden so well
Even she couldn't tell.

Convincing herself
"There's nothing wrong just doing me",
Living life,
Fighting for the chance,
That maybe
Someday
Someone
Will actually see
The true her
but until then,
She hides away.

His Heart Speaks

He without her.
Her without him.
Now they without them.
Now look at the outcome in the end,
No at last please don't pretend
I love her
I love her
Love her to the end.

Human Perspective

Only person who you can
rely on is yourself.
People will always
Flake on you,
Hurt you,
Give up on you.

But can you really rely on you?
Didn't you flake on you?
Not completing goals.
Didn't you hurt you?
Not valuing who you are?
Didn't you give up on you?
Letting your dream go.

Reality is we are humans.
Humans make mistakes.
Even to ourselves.

When you don't flake on you
When you don't hurt you
When you don't give up on you.
They won't either.

Inconsolable

When I saw you,
I saw the pain in you.
I saw the pain in your eyes.
I saw the pain in your soul.

An intensified first night.
I became your pain,
You became my pain,
We became one soul.

I wanted to save you from yourself.
I wanted to save you from them.
I wanted to save you from your pain.

For I could see the control.
For I could see the manipulation.
A grown man living for others,
A man making mistakes to please everyone.

I wanted you to see more to life.
I wanted you to see your value.
I wanted you to see your worth.
How much more you deserved.

I thought you were the one,
That would ease my pain.
The one that would finally love me,
The one that would protect me.

I gave you everything,
I gave you my heart,
I gave you being a fool,
I gave you my trust.

Inconsolable (Cont'd)

But instead of love,
You abused my love.
Love for granted you took,
Stranded you left me.

Stranded in my tears,
Stranded in my pain.
Stranded in my thoughts,
Stranded in my heart.

Broken was my soul.
Lost was my soul.
Lost to your lies,
Lost to your desires.

You lost me and
didn't even stop.
Now, pieces I pickup
Unaided.

Never thought the man
who said a bullet he would take,
would be responsible for
the emotional bullet I would take.

Never knew you
would be responsible,
For the death of my heart.
For the death of my soul.

Darkness fills inside me.
Darkness has overtaken me.
Feeling of pure love,
Tarnished to pure hate.

Inconsolable (Cont'd)

A hate that wants you,
Burning inside like me.
A pain that wants revenge
Wants you to feel what I felt.

You got what you wanted.
What you wanted wasn't me.
Had the chance to love me,
Protect me and choose me
But you let me die instead.

When you left me,
You left the pain in me.
You left the pain in my eyes.
You left the pain in my soul.

Inspired Spirit

A muse of inspiration.
A muse of light.
Who would have thought?
That you could be so bright

Sitting with anticipation
Of your next creation.
Hoping that when paper meets pen.
The union becomes more than just pretend.

Not just a pencil waiting,
For the next eraser but,
An everlasting ink stain,
In this place call life.

Never to erase the mistakes,
But to look the design,
Of every single moment,
And every yielded turn.

Who could have thought?
That you could be so bright.
A muse of light!
A muse of inspiration.

Jaded

Loving and giving
Giving and loving.

You keep loving
And it seems
You keep losing.

You keep giving.
And not feel
It in return.

You have loved.
You have given.
Sacrificed yourself,
In order to love them.

But now can you trust
to be loved?

KNEW ART, NEW HEART

He never knew ART,
Until he had a broken heart.

See the pain he now possess is seen
On the stroke of each
Brush,

His passion in the line of each
Drawing,

His fear in the shadow of each
Painting.

In his mind is the key to his deliverance.
In his hands are the release of his medicine.
In this eyes are the secrets he deeply hides.

He never knew he had art.
He never knew he had a heart.

Until he had a broken heART,
He never knew ART.

Legal Thoughts

I always seem to put myself into these predicaments. I'm legal now, I'm eighteen years, starting college and I've fallen in like already. Oh no not love. Not so quick but a major like. With a sexual attraction so big. I could just burst with a deep look from his eyes.

I believe it's all a lie but something is telling me it's true. How do i overcome this evil spirit of deceit and eventually pain? I try to pull away but it grows. Stronger and stronger and mesmerizes me into an unconscious feeling of lust.

Just being with him. No ties. No strings attached satisfies a part of me with no regrets but makes me wonder what he thinks of me. Does he really respect me or is it a front? Is it private? Between him and I or everyone?

Is it really a way to receive pleasure without the circle around me caving in with the thoughts of minds around you thinking you are stupid to fall for game? Will it all be over by the strike of dawn and never be seen again? To even believe the words that come from his sweet lips. It's hard to trust someone.

When all you want is someone to be discrete. Where you don't have to worry about people in your business. The pressure of relationship. The problems and heartaches of another half. Just a friend with benefits. Someone to talk to, hang out just chill. Could it be? I hope so.

Love Imposter

Some people say
Love is blind.
But I say
Love see's straight
Through the faults and binds.

Some people say
Love hurts.
But I say
There's no way.

See the reality of it all is,
Everyone wants love.
To be loved.
To love.

So when the pain arises
When the hurt is so deep
It wasn't love that caused it.

Love was just an innocent bystander
From the criminal who came
To destroy what love had bound.

Lost Soul

Looking at the Master Plan,
My master plan,
With things to plan
The way I can.

I need to get it
How I can get it,
My wants my needs
No time to breathe.

I got this need.
But then this need
Tends to make me
Deserted.
In helpless places.

Now I don't want to look
At other people's faces.
So I hide and cry
And ask Jesus why?

I need help fast
So I pray and fast
Fast and pray
And say
Jesus I'm, yours.

No one else can I turn to
And still feel victorious
Because you're so glorious
Giving me the victory
Over my biggest enemy,

Lost Soul (Cont'd)

ME

So I pray through
My temptation.
Guide me through
My lust and frustration.

Lust of my flesh.
Lust of my eyes.
I put down my pride
And humbly ask.

Equip me with spirits fruit
With power and strength
It's time to be bound, only
To you,
For the victory is mine, only
Through you.

Misguided Judgement

I am not good enough.
I am not old enough.
I just don't know enough.

Who said?
You said.
I said.
They said.

I made too many mistakes.
I made them now its's too late.

I'm a failure.
I'm so stupid.

You told me
And I believed
They told me
And I repeated

But now I know
I was misguided
Misguided by your judgement
Misguided by their judgement

Guided was my judgement
From your misguiding judgement.
Never again.

Neglected Abandonment

You told me you were leaving
I took it for a joke.
What I thought was pretend
Was really not a joke.

So absent you went
And abandoned I felt.

What was I going to do?
What was I going to say?
To my children,
To my co-workers,
To the people at the church?

I felt resentment.
I felt agony.

Neglected was my name
Abandonment was the game
I don't want to play that game
You sailed away.

Obscure Liberation

A spiritual eclipse,
Created to bring darkness,
Designed to develop,
Direction it will provide.

In the darkness is the silence,
In the darkness is reflection,
The darkness may seem obscure,
yet through it liberation.

A spiritual eclipse,
Darkness created.
Experience of dawning.
Dawning of a new day.

Phoenix

I want a life,
I want to be alive.

Living constantly,
Constantly living.

Living with regret,
Regretfully living.
Am I really living?

Drake said it best.
Everybody dies,
But not everybody lives.

I want to live,
I want to be alive.

So like the phoenix
I Rise.

Left are my ashes of pride
Renewed authenticity

Reborn to live the true me.

Queen Status

I don't have status

I don't have influence

How can I be a queen?

You don't need status

You don't need influence

Inheritance is yours queen.

Your father has status

Your father has influence

He created you in his image.

Whenever you doubt

Whenever you question

Always remember you have Queen Status.

Real False

Flowing to the beat of the drum
That leads to destruction,
Following the streams of life
That leads to death.
It's calm and seductive.
A façade of beautification and joy
Yet the turbulence inside,
Collides with the calm
And you awake;
BOOM! ...
Reality!!

Rested Peace

Rest in Peace
Not when you're dead
But during the time that you're
Most alive.

Peace that surpasses
Is there understanding?
For those who seek His face
There's a special holy place.

On a hill it was erased
Impurity, imperfection
Trying to be a reflection
of the perfect peace
Shackles released.

Sense the understanding
Peace that surpasses
Spirit most alive
When peace is rested
Abundantly in you.

Sag Tamed

Beyonce said it best
"I was in love with a sagittarius"
But this love story is double sagalicious

Loving you is like loving myself.
More than mating of souls.
More like flaming of twins.

We are so different but so alike
Modern Romeo meets Juliet
Country Boy meets City Girl.

You in your world
I in my world
Now we in our world.

To you a whole new world.
To me a different world
To them a forbidden world.

A world that somehow evolved.
A world that was never planned.
A world that we never intended

They said it started wrong.
How does it feel right?
Things just feel right
With the one they feel right with.

Sag Tamed (Cont'd)

A world that just exploded.
Within each others eyes is
The reflection of each other's soul

The one you were chasing
Was a missing part of you.
The one I was chasing
Was a missing part of me.

I wanted it to end.
You wouldn't let me go.
Now a new beginning
How will it end?

More than flaming of twins.
More than mating of souls
Loving myself is loving you.

I'm in love with a Sagittarius
You're in love with a Sagittarius.

Served Notice

You try to make me fall.
You try to make me cry.
You try to push me over the edge.
You want to see me dead.

But that would be murder.
So instead of pulling the trigger,
You provoke me to commit suicide,
Knowing that you can't kill me on your own.

Planted seeds that turn into thorn bushes.
Pricking me on my way.
Planted seeds that turns into wild trees
Roots and branches so wide,
Causing me to bruise, causing me to stumble.

I should be crying.

The pricking of my fingers.
The branches hitting my face.
The bruising on my knees.
The stumbling of my feet.

I have something greater.
Something in me that is greater.
Greater is he that is in me.
Than he that is in the world.

I will not fall.
I will not cry.
I will not go over the edge.
You will not see me dead.

Served Notice (Cont'd)

Suicide will not be my end.

Planted are my own seeds.
Those thorn bushes. Turn into roses
Those branches. Turn into shelter
Those stumbling roots. Turn into stepping stones.

Similarly Different

Sometimes you feel so close to me.
Like sharing the same though.
Breathing the same breath.

Sometimes you feel so far away.
Like distance waves of understanding
Beating hearts apart.

We are so much alike,
Nevertheless such difference.
Could be unequally yoked.
Could be heavenly matched.

What a difference!
From fine dining to deer meat,
Fishing on the lake to messages & reflexology.

The same intensity and burning fire,
Passion so deep in it we would drown.
Is this love our heavenly place or holy hell?
It is time that will only tell.

Tell

I wish someone had told me
No, no, no
I mean really told me
All I heard was don't do it

Why?
Because I said so

Why?
Because the bible says so

Why?
Because it's wrong!

Bottom line no questions asked
Just don't do it.

So I did it, age 14, yep I did it
And it was terrible
I was so scared
and it hurt

I wish someone had told me
Really told me.
Even when they found out
They still didn't tell me.

So why'd you do it?
I don't know

Don't do it no more

Tell (Cont'd)

Why?
Because I said so!

Here we go again,
Yep I did it again,
And again and again
Until it was part of.
Part of the routine

A part that was slowly killing me.

But I wish someone had told me
Really told me
So now I tell you
Don't do it
Why?
Because it kills you

It kills your mind
It kills your soul
It kills your connection with
The ultimate spiritual sensation
So don't do it
Not yet
Not until him you have met.

Thinking Thoughts

What am I feeling?

What am I Thinking?

A lot but cannot say

What I'm feeling

What I'm thinking

Cause what I'm thinking

Got me thinking.

This, That, It… Deal!

This, That, It
Everybody has a
This, That, It

This is too much.
That is so frustrating.
It is overwhelming.

Whatever is your This.
Whatever is your That.
Whatever is your It.

Don't Just Dwell on it
We all have something
Something has us all.

Deal with that.
Deal with this.
Deal with it.

Uninhabited

Love don't live here anymore
Did love ever live here?

For we are so Blinded by
Consummation and the
Consumption of an
Emotional burning feeling
Deep within our soul, We
Desire to turn this hot,
Speechless sensation into Love
BUT,

Love don't live here anymore
Did love ever live here?

For we are Bounded by
Emotional entrapment
Deep within our minds, We
Desire to turn this brief
Motionless moment into Love
BUT

Love don live here anymore
Did love ever live here?

For we are Bargaining the
Everlasting elements of our
Well needed Essence
What is Patience? What is kind?

Uninhabited (Cont'd)

When all you need is to be Fine!?
Not really,
But in our minds we have
Characterized the beautification of the
Outward Appearance
Forsaking all inner developments of the
Characterization of the Spirits Fruit
BUT

Love don't live here anymore
Truth. Love never lived here!

For we content ourselves with
Unkindness, impatience,
Rude attitudes are justified as being
Directedness.
Self Indulgence- the Predication of the
Deterioration of our existence
Don't think for a minute
If you ever did wrong that
Love will love you, the same
Unconditionally,
At least man's Love
BUT

Love don't live here anymore
How can love live here?

Uninhabited (Cont'd)

For if it did
Wrongdoings would not be the
Building blocks of your hierarchy
No sense to think of harm,
Even to your enemy
Not just the one you want to see
Succeed.
Protection will be your Weapon
Trust will be your Shield
Hope will be your Sword
Perseverance will be your Armor.

Love don't live here anymore!
Love never lived here!

For God gave us the pattern of Love
Sacrificing his only son.
Will you give so I can live?
Having Faith, Giving All, Being Wise,
Did you know you'll still be
Nothing
Because you lack
Something
Love!

Love don't live here!
Love never lived here!
When?
Will love live here

Unfelt

There was a time
When all I felt was
Anger!
The thought of you
Made me sick to my soul.
I wondered what I had
Done?
To get involved with a
Fool.
I wasn't even a fool in love,
More like a desperate heart,
Longing for love.
Thinking if I made one move
You'll want me.
Now I'm lonely
Fool played me for a fool
Now instead of anger
I'm just numb...

Unspoken Unity

The eyes,
Tells the story of the soul's fury.
I love you
Well I don't really love you, my soul do.

In that moment nothing matters
Spirit commits. Mind oblivious to time.

Time stands still for a moment
The moment to be intertwined.

Uniting Mind, body and spirit.
Become one. Explodes.

Separating what was once united.

Wasted time

Wasting time.

Living in yesterday.
Thinking about all the things,
That could've, should've happen.

Wasting time.

Living in tomorrow.
Thinking about all the things,
That I want and need to do.

Wasting time. Forgetting

If there was a yesterday
If there will be a tomorrow,
That there is a today.

Live in today.
Doing all the things today.
Loving all the people today.

For soon tomorrow,
Will be today,
Today will be yesterday.

Stop wasting time.

Zealous Exhalation

I come to the finale of my soliloquies. Through these writings expressed to you are many private moments and transparent thoughts. The journey of expression has been on a roller coaster of collected sentiments. Endured through the years are the ramifications of decisions and interacting with individuals. It is often easy to critique others and make judgements about people and have no inclination of the battles they fight every day. Everyone has feelings, thoughts and emotions. As a human being it is impossible to not go through situations. You are human which means you have endured trial and tribulations. Many of these in your mind. In your thoughts. Sometimes people are unable to express their thoughts and may cope in a negative manner. They may drink excessively, become codependent on drugs and sexual acts.

Overconsumption of food, socially withdrawing from others, overworking or avoidance behaviors. It may not seem and feel like we have control but we do have control. We possess the internal response of our external stimuli. We do not always get it

Zealous Exhalation (Cont'd)

right and it does not always come easy but we can do it. You can do it! I did it! I myself have coped in negative ways but I have pushed through my fears and barriers. It is ok to have thoughts, we just do not want to stay in the place of our bad moments or negative thinking. Writing has been one of my mechanisms on how to cope and expressing my thoughts. You are not alone. Whatever thought or feelings may come your way someone else has experienced it and someone else has overcame. We can shift our thinking. There are so many methods to have a healthy emotional lifestyle. You just have to seek the methods that work best for you and that will generate a positive and productive result. Release your feelings in a constructive way. I am not sure what you may believe but I am a believer that we are spirits and that we do not battle against flesh and blood but the battle is in our spirit, it is in our mind. We have the power to throw away thinking. I am reminded of Paul's words from the book of Philippians; Chapter 4 verse 8: "Whatever is true, whatever is noble, whatever is right, whatever is pure, whatever is

Zealous Exhalation (Cont'd)

lovely, whatever is admirable—if anything is excellent or praiseworthy—think about such things. "Bad things happen. Good things happen. It does not always equate to a person being good or bad. Good things happen to good and bad people just like bad things happen to both. We cannot get stuck in our works and what we did but we can transform our attitude and the things we experience today. Everyone generates a wave of thought. As we think of these things we can exude great energy. We can move through life with zealous exhalation.

Finally Exhale!

Made in the USA
Columbia, SC
29 November 2020